ENTREPRENEUR

THE JOURNEY OF A LIFETIME

Shailesh K Dash
www.shaileshkdash.com

Published by Shailesh K Dash
Amazon & Kindle Publishing

Available for purchase online at www.amazon.com,
Kindle Edition
Available in paperback and online Kindle format

Find out more at www.shaileshkdash.com

Dedicated to Lord Jagannath

Gratitude to my parents (Prassanna and Rebati) and grandparents for helping me imbibe extraordinary qualities and for being my Ultimate Life Coach

I am also incredibly thankful to my family Andreea, Shailaja, Amaiya, SwetaPadma, Sagarika, and Subhada for their love and support.

ENTREPRENEUR
THE JOURNEY OF A LIFETIME

CONTENTS

FOREWORD	H. E. DATO DR AMIN ABDULLAH
INTRODUCTION	THE JOURNEY OF A LIFETIME
CHAPTER ONE	LOVE AND COMPASSION
CHAPTER TWO	LIVE YOUR PASSION
CHAPTER THREE	HUNGER AND SUFFERING
CHAPTER FOUR	SETTING GOALS
CHAPTER FIVE	TAKE RISKS TO GROW
CHAPTER SIX	ENTREPRENEURSHIP
CHAPTER SEVEN	PARTNERSHIPS
CHAPTER EIGHT	ENTREPRENEURSHIP'S REWARDS AND PITFALLS
CHAPTER NINE	MANAGING GROWTH
CHAPTER TEN	FINANCING
CHAPTER ELEVEN	MANAGING CHANGES
CHAPTER TWELVE	HOW TO START A NEW BUSINESS
CHAPTER THIRTEEN	POWERFUL HEALTH PRACTICES FOR ENTREPRENEURS
CHAPTER FOURTEEN	START-UP
CLOSING NOTES	

FOREWORD

H. E. DATO DR AMIN ABDULLAH

Entrepreneurs are brave adventurers.

They risk everything, putting their faith in what they believe to be brilliant ideas. They step forth—out into the unknown, not certain of success, frequently facing imposing obstacles, encountering insurmountable challenges and yet, never giving up.

I first met Shailesh back in 2005 and have followed his progress over the last fifteen years from Kuwait to Dubai and his forays into Singapore and Malaysia. I have watched as Shailesh's Lifetime Journey has unfolded, and as I read his story, I see in it the reflections of every entrepreneur: concentrate on one thing and do it with all your passion.

Shailesh has compiled a short and inspiring diary of the lessons that he learned along his way, sharing his personal challenges and business experience, and today, he stands tall amongst those who have fought and won the entrepreneurship battle, not once, but many times.

Listen and learn from him, for these lessons were bought at a high price of time, commitment, and above all, passion.

Keep on going, Shailesh!

Amin.

THE JOURNEY OF A LIFETIME

Visiting home many years on, I reflect on my humble beginnings, sitting beside the beach and gazing out to sea. What a journey it turned out to be! I could never have imagined the wonders and places that I would visit and the diversity of people that I would meet.

Being an entrepreneur at heart, this strong desire was born in me as a child; moving from one city to another turned into moving from one country to another and onward to creating companies that would change many people's lives.

The journey of an entrepreneur is an all-consuming one, and while it is not for everyone, for those who choose to walk this lonely road, entrepreneurism has many rewards as well as challenges and surprises.

It is an all-or-nothing game. You have to give it everything you've got and keep on going long after everyone else has given up and gone home. More than anything, it is about having great dreams and staying focused, and that one mysterious ingredient—the commitment to never ever give up, no matter what. Learning to pivot, learning to flow, and learning that a big mistake can be the magical moment that creates the success of the company are all part of the journey.

Above all, remember that entrepreneurship is all about customers. Focus on making a product that will make your customer happy; this can help make a profit and turn you into a very successful entrepreneur.

My journey is far from done and I have paused to pen these lines so that you may be encouraged and inspired to take up the challenge of becoming an entrepreneur and experiencing the freedom that comes with the responsibility.

I wish you all the success in your endeavors and hope my thoughts help you along your way.

Shailesh K Dash

CHAPTER ONE

LOVE AND COMPASSION

I firmly believe that no two lives are the same and that everybody's experience is personal. The principles of life, hopefully, remain the same for all of us along the way. Although I am not a guru, saint, life coach, trainer, or somebody who can tell you what you need to do in your life, I can certainly share my thoughts and experiences to help you along your journey.

As I advance in years, it is much easier to look back upon how my childhood, college days, and early working life have shaped me and formed my views. These experiences have helped me become the person I am today. The way I have come to see things in life, it is important to remember how you started because sometimes we don't understand how to connect the dots; but, if you know your origin and embrace your own story, it will lead you in your future.

I was born into a middle-class family in India, and because my father worked in the public sector, we would frequently move from one city to another. My childhood learning was not all found in the classroom, and I believe it was the extracurricular education that most helped to shape my personality. Even though I did not realize this until later in life, these experiences had a great effect on my professional life and career.

At an early age, I learned to have the deepest respect for my elders and teachers; this helped me later on when I joined the workforce, understanding that following the requests and directions provided by my bosses and seniors was in my own interests, and so, listening to my bosses and seniors is probably why I was always loved by them and this helped me to grow quickly.

My childhood memories, on the other hand, were all about moving. With each move, I would have to enroll in a different school, and, so, I learned how to adapt to different cultures and communities quickly. I met new classmates and encountered different teaching methods and discovered the importance of diversity in learning and not just to depend on a set-way of studying. I managed to find ways to learn not only from books but also from the journey; these constantly changing environments and new classmates instilled in me a spirit of independence at a young age. I was committed to finding alternative ways to learn, not just from the textbooks and classes but also from extracurricular activities.

Prayer and meditation were encouraged in my family and became a deep and rich part of who I am today. This foundation has helped me significantly in stressful situations and has allowed me to concentrate on the bigger picture. Many begin life with prayer and meditation and give it up along the way; however, personally, I have learned that this is an essential pillar in life.

Mistakes, oh mistakes. We all make them. I was lucky because from my earliest recollection I was encouraged to try my hand at new things, which can obviously lead to mistakes; the key, however, was to learn from each mistake and not repeat it— the same holds true even today.

Growing up, my grandparents and, later, my mother ensured that we rigorously followed a routine based upon discipline and punctuality. They all had strict guidelines about timing and daily activities, and this is something that I have always adhered to; I continue these traditions by being very structured in my actions and thought processes. It helps bring regularity to my schedule, sleeping and waking, going to the gym, and being at work at a certain time. I am always reminded of the significance of this rhythm by the Sun—it rules all the planets and our days and nights are determined by when it rises and sets; it is consistent. It is at the center of our solar system and provides life-giving light to our world. Moreover, the way our Earth revolves around it determines the timeline we follow. Its consistent rising and setting has remained the same all through the centuries and will continue to stay so. This is something we can try to strive for in our lives: to become consistent—with our quality of life, work output, and commitments. And as is the consistency of the Sun in providing us with life, so our lives will be enriched by consistency.

As with all young boys, our fathers are our greatest examples. Mine taught me the virtues of compassion and kindness, either through his teachings to me or his interactions with others. He believed that being kind was essential and took the time to instill this quality in me.

These childhood experiences have formed who I am, and today, they have helped me in leading a diverse team, working within groups, and creating organizations that have contributed to the economy in various ways, including providing job opportunities for many.

These lessons are worth repeating.

Discipline and being disciplined is invaluable to me as I manage a team of people hailing from different backgrounds and cultures. I depend upon being compassionate and kind to everybody. Not to forget that early independence which led me to get tasks completed without being reliant on others.

My hope is that you will keep these lessons in mind for your journey towards becoming an independent and kind entrepreneur.

LEARNING/ADVICE

If you are going through a difficult time, don't worry about what God has in store for you.
Believe in the process and keep up your discipline and hard work and never give up.

Nobody can stop you from achieving anything that you wish to put your mind to.

CHAPTER TWO

LIVE YOUR PASSION

You must live your passion. This is another very important lesson in my life, where, as I look back, I find that so many things I had learnt that helped shape my thought process and personality, ultimately benefiting me much later in life and helping me to connect the dots.

Leaving your family and going to study in another city can be quite strenuous. Fast forward to my graduation, I got the chance to move to yet another city for my studies. There, staying in a hostel with students of different ages and cultural backgrounds, I was able to cement relationships that are still going strong today. My parents and grandparents wanted me to pursue an education in the field of Science; however, I was more inclined towards learning Economics. Although this disappointed them, I decided to take this step and work hard to prove to my family that it was worth it. With hard work and determination, I was able to prove myself; I was determined that I wouldn't fail in anything that I would set my mind to, and, even if I did, I would get back up on my feet and continue on my journey. My dedication helped me to strive hard throughout my years of study and overcome the fact that I had switched fields.

Here are some of the lessons that college taught me:

Moving from Science to Economics was not easy and mastering a different subject meant I had to work harder and change my entire thinking process, but it gave me the confidence that I could manage and master any subject. I think a lot of that credit goes to my schooling and my teachers and parents as well as my resolve that I would not accept to fail in anything I do.

To be very frank, the only thing that mattered to me was that I did very well so that I could prove to my family that my decision to shift from the only subject they wanted me to pursue (Science) was right.

I wanted to prove that my decision to move to Economics and write my own career path was indeed a good one. For that to happen, I really concentrated in the first year to make sure that I got my basics in Economics clear. It helped me a great deal in the following years while I was doing my MBA and even later in my role as a research analyst.

The following have been my learnings from my graduation years which have helped me up until today:
1) Change is constant.
2) You should never be afraid to start or pursue something that you are passionate about. Never be afraid to start something that you like.
3) If you have the passion to learn something, you can always succeed with hard work, sacrifice, and discipline. My earlier success gave me the confidence that I could achieve anything I wanted if I put my heart and soul into it, and I was ready to make sacrifices and maintain discipline. Much later in time, it was this that inspired me when I was trying to reinvent my life and took the step to leave my job and start my own business with a new team and new partners.
4) Staying in hostels with students from different cultures and backgrounds helped me learn from them, gain respect for them, and work together to create a more cohesive environment. Although we might have had our differences within those three years, it would always melt away. We managed to create a genuine camaraderie

and create a bond that has helped us keep in touch all these years later.
5) Making sacrifices is something that comes along with the journey, no matter how young or old you are. Even though they might all seem insignificant now, sacrificing delicious meals and the luxury that I could avail at my grandfather's house for the not-so-great food at my hostel was something that allowed me to spend more time studying and preparing for my exams. This proved to be quite fruitful as I graduated at the top of my class in Economics and Mathematics among 915 students in Utkal University, which is one of the most prestigious and oldest universities in India. The sense of satisfaction made me realize that my decision for rewriting the course of my career was correct and it only served to prove that with hard work, patience, and sacrifices could help you succeed in your endeavors. I can remember many times I would make sacrifices so that I could spend more time reading books, prepare for exams, or learn from my friends.
6) Never be afraid to take actions and fail at something that you are passionate about.

They say that if you don't take any action, although you will avoid failure, you will also not progress in your life. As many successful mentors would say, the only way you can learn, and grow is by making mistakes while unapologetically trying to follow your passion.

LEARNING/ADVICE

Don't be afraid of change or failure.
Both are important to grow in life.

It's very important to live your passion even if that would mean sacrificing and failing a few times, but your will to achieve and your willingness to go that extra mile will always bring about positive changes and success to your life.

CHAPTER THREE

HUNGER AND SUFFERING

Another very important aspect of learning, and later maybe unlearning feature of my adult life, was pursuing an MBA degree in New Delhi. I had no experience of living in a mega city like New Delhi, and this was totally new for a comparatively introverted person like me. With almost no friends or family there initially, my uncle got a job in the city and moved there with my aunt. I, subsequently, got to know some other distant family members living there, which proved very helpful.

Living in a big city with no family safety net! Nothing in my previous experience of five different schools and staying in the hostel at college could have prepared me for what came next. I found myself left to study and fend for myself with no real support. Here, I would develop some of my best friendships with my fellow classmates who hailed from different parts of India; all of whom dreamed of becoming successful in their lives. For the very first time, the sense of survival set in among all of us who migrated to New Delhi from other states, causing us to group together and look for ways to stick together for the next two years. While it seemed to be an inconsequential thing for those who had travelled since their younger days, it was very different not to stay in a protective environment like the college hostel.

I guess that was, in a way, my first lesson in management which helped me when I became a manager. A lot of the stuff that we learned then had to be unlearned later when we joined the corporate world, and much of that stuff may not even be valid anymore. There are certain principles which have worked well for me, and I think, if they are implemented in the correct way, they could help everyone that aspires to hold a senior position in the corporate world. I say this because those who are already higher up probably already follow these principles.

1) Management, in simple terms, means to manage or be in-charge of resources—be it people, systems, or capital. To me, the word Management explains itself and it means manage + men + tactically:

MANAGEMENT = MANAGE + MEN + T
MANAGE + MEN AND WOMEN + TACTICALLY

And to become a manager, we need to understand what it means, manager is to manage + R (resources) which could be people, systems, or capital.

MANAGER = MANAGE + R

2) The suffering we had to undergo everyday just to survive in the mega city alone during that time and complete our studies with the least amount of support from anywhere would help me survive and appreciate the learnings I had during those days. Therefore, please always remember that if you are undergoing pain and suffering to fulfil your passions, that's because God wants you to be strong and not waiver in real life in times of difficulties.
3) Your passion and hunger to achieve can encourage you to work harder without the fear of failing. Countless successful individuals have gone down this path; many of them have outlined this in their autobiographies. It's the hunger and suffering which helps a man to think differently and work harder without the fear of losing. Study successful individuals and read their books, and you will see that this is the case in many instances.

With our internship opportunities during our MBA degree, it was finally time to apply our skills in the real world and this became an interesting time in my career.

My first opportunity was a two-month internship with ABB company in Bangalore. This mega city welcomed me with wide open arms; here, there were no batchmates to spend time with and I had a totally new city to discover. Again, I did not know anybody except some relatives from my uncle's side of the family.

The first summer that I was an intern at ABB, it was not really what I had wished for. However, later, that stint would come in handy as I went to work in a similar workplace at Daewoo Motors, a large automotive company. Large factory set ups are very different from a corporate office—working life demands understanding and I got plenty of first-hand experience in the same, particularly being present during a strike where I was stuck in the factory and was able to learn how the leadership and HR team were able to navigate and create solutions to maintain order and ensure our safety.

Connecting the dots in life can sometimes be a strange process. Similar things happened when I went to work in a Treasury function at the Daewoo Factory. This was when I realized what God had in store for me and was what I had been trained in, and that I had acquired the experience to manage adversity.

In today's world, negative things impact us very quickly and we can tend to give them far more attention than the good things that happen in our lives. As an entrepreneur, it is essential that we concentrate on the many good things and remember that the negative is simply an opportunity to learn what does not work and try again.

As a 22-year-old, everything was new to me and there was so much to learn. The real grinding came when I started working as a management trainee. My experience was very similar to that of the characters from the book *Monkey Business* which I read much later when I was in Kuwait. The following thoughts summarize my experience as a trainee:

1) When you start your work as a trainee, the fundamentals of your finance/marketing/HR are very important irrespective of your field of specialization. The corporate world is very different, and the way it works cannot be taught at any business school, so most importantly, ready to unlearn almost everything you have learnt there. You must be adaptive as everyday will present its own set of

challenges. Drawing from my own personal experience, I had to work long hours (18-hour days) for weeks on end; sometimes, even on weekends. Although this made me feel physically drained, I was able to strengthen my knowledge about how an enterprise functions over the years, my analytical bent of mind, good presentation skills, excellent Excel skills, and most importantly, problem-solving skills meant being able to do almost everything that my seniors threw at me. On many days, that meant that I would work from 8 a.m. in the morning until 2 a.m. the next day, for weeks on end. I must say that while doing all this, I might have hated my work life, but around three years down the line, I had learnt so much and strengthened my working knowledge. This enabled me to independently conduct business development which helped me climb up the corporate ladder much faster and made my bosses always appreciate my value.

2) I learnt that, in the corporate world, we always need to maintain our value which means that if your company seeks to acquire somebody with your skill set and experience in the market then you charge 10-20 percent less than the market. This means they can never let you go and you will ride out the market vagaries. You will

always be loved by your company and bosses because they have no better alternative.
3) If you want to become an entrepreneur, it is always better to work with a start-up or a small organization where you can play an integral part in the organization's growth and get involved in everyday tasks; this is, however, unlikely in large organizations where you get compartmentalized into performing only a set number of functions. I used to be sad during the initial stages of my career, as I never got to work in a large corporate organization, except to some extent maybe Daewoo; however, again, after connecting the dots, it was most helpful for me to lead independent businesses and establish new businesses because I learned that there is no work that I would ever think was beneath me. I would always be ready to work hard and use my skill set to do whatever would help in making small start-up entities become success stories.
4) As a trainee, I learned how to maintain relationships and improve them which surely goes a long way when developing a business.
5) Based on my experience, I can say that you should never avoid or neglect any tasks no matter what size or shape they come in.

However, at the same time, you should be firm, honest, and disciplined. This is always appreciated by the clients and seniors and makes them view you as a reliable and valuable employee. In my experience, all I can say is, never neglect work.

6) Speaking the truth helps in the long run.

LEARNING/ADVICE

It's the hunger to achieve and the lessons you learn with failure, rejection, and suffering which will be the steppingstones for your future success.

Don't get sad or disheartened; believe in the lessons you would learn in life because of those failures and suffering and use those experiences as your strength to bring positive changes to your work and personal life.

CHAPTER FOUR

SETTING GOALS

We are a product of the teachings of our parents and teachers, our background, as well as the environment that we have grown up in. Every decision that we take at any stage in our lives has consequences; therefore, we must be ready to face the consequences regardless of whether they are positive or not.

For instance, I was at the top of my class during graduation; however, I did not choose to appear for the Civil Services exam in India, which was the path that most of the graduates in Economics chose. Instead, I decided to pursue my degree in Management Studies which was, unlike my family members, a decision to pursue a career in the private sector.

That was a choice I made, and I had to live with it and prove to everybody in the family that it was the right one.

You cannot grow without sacrifices, but it is important to never lose sight of the goal you have set for yourself. For me, personally, I had to leave the security of my home, miss my mother's amazing cooking, my father's love and protection, endure erratic sleep cycles, stay back late to finish my work at the office, live on average-quality meals, share my room with a roommate, and even be unable to take some time out for myself. No matter the challenges I faced, I never forgot the path I had chosen for myself and never lost sight of the big picture. I began by setting smaller, achievable targets whenever things seemed overwhelming which helped me to efficiently gauge my progress.

It is important to set goals and targets as early as possible so that you can leave enough time to plan and execute them. It can help you endure the hardships you may face on your journey.

I cannot emphasize the importance of goals in life enough, and it does not matter which motivational or business book you read, you will find that they always begin with its vision, mission, and goals before anything else. Therefore, if you have not set goals for yourself yet, you should do that now. It is never too late to set your life on the right path. We all owe it to ourselves and our families to do it so that we can find the right purpose of our existence.

As I said before, change is the only constant in life. However, it is only a good thing if it leads one to break away from bad practices. I believe that physical activities and maintaining a healthy lifestyle not only helps our body but also our mind and, in due course, it helps us to refine our thinking processes. It allows us to sweat off the pressures of our hectic daily life and makes us feel pumped up so that we can carry on with our routine. Back in the day, I did not have much time or money to be able to go to a gym, but I still ensured that I would go out on long walks. Even today, I make time to go work out in the gym as it helps me feel determined to achieve my physical and life goals. We may face many disappointments in life but the way we handle them will ultimately define us.

LEARNING/ADVICE

Setting a goal is very important and, without it, life has no value.

I believe that once we try to achieve something in life and give our 100% towards it, and keep our thoughts always centered around the same, we will most likely be able to achieve it.

While on your journey towards success, it is important that you always look forward to the future rather than looking backwards.

I strongly believe that we all create our own reality.

CHAPTER FIVE

TAKE RISKS TO GROW

In this chapter, I would like to share some of the tough decisions that I had to make over the course of my career. Despite working hard for almost six and a half years in India, I was unable to make real progress as far as my vision and goals for my career were concerned. I was determined to start my own venture but owing to the market conditions and the exposure being received, I was unable to save enough or plan for any initial ventures while I was there. Therefore, I made the difficult decision to move out of India and find my true calling. Although the move was not easy, my ambition to move helped make it all a worthwhile risk to take. We, as budding entrepreneurs, must strive to make a difference in our lives and the communities around us. I must say that the decision was, eventually, a positive one. Moving to a different country was not easy, but with my ambition and goal ahead of me, I knew that I had to strive to make it a reality. Leading a mediocre life can be quite tiresome; therefore, it is important for all of us to try our best and make a difference to our lives. And this will only be possible when we achieve our goals.

Travelling to Kuwait was the first time that I had travelled outside India, and though it was an international destination, I did not feel that far from home; this was because many people living there were from my home country. Following this trip and the many more I was fortunate enough to have around the world, I was able to adjust my mindset and worldview. I experienced different cultures and acquired greater appreciation for them. I became more accepting, flexible, and more receptive. I learned how to be more humane and compassionate and was able to change my approach in order to build a successful business.

I consider my travels to be among the most valuable experiences I could have for my future development in the times to come. So much so that I can confidently say today that I would not be the person I am without these travels and meeting and learning from many kind and learned souls around the world.

By travelling to and working in Kuwait, I was able to achieve financial independence. I was blessed enough to be working for a company with great leadership; they provided me with independence to evolve my business acumen and start delivering top-notch results for their company. The healthy work culture in the organization provided its employees with an opportunity to grow. It also provided me with first-hand experience in understanding how efficient leadership can help a company progress in the market.

This was only possible because of the economic environment that prevailed in the Gulf and around the world during that time, along with a very positive leadership team at the organization, that provided serious hard-working professionals with growth opportunities.

On three separate occasions, I experienced how young, dynamic, and motivated leadership with a good work culture can help businesses grow faster—twice in India and once in Kuwait.

I would summarize my learnings as follows:

1) There is no substitute for international experience.
2) You must try and join a young team with dynamic leadership as it can help improve your skill set and enhance your overall development.
3) When you scale the corporate ladder, your soft skills will matter the most. No school in the world prepares you for that. Even so, you must try and incorporate those skills in

your life as soon as possible as it becomes a defining aspect of you as an entrepreneur; you must learn the hard skills. It is, however, important to remember that this is not a substitute for hard work; your soft skills, ethics, and value system are something that will help you to progress in your career in the long-term.

4) Although this may seem like a given, it is very important for you to give your best to your organization and be true to yourself. Your results will only be a reflection of your efforts.

5) As an organization grows, there will always be office politics. You must never get involved in these as it will eat away your precious work time and hinder the progression of your career. Instead, you must spend time on yourself and with your family; you can even work on improving your skill set. It is always advisable not to get involved in things that are unproductive or non-beneficial for your career.

6) Do not be afraid to take risks if you think it would help your organization; however, you must ensure that you always discuss the risks with your seniors and take their advice.

7) Nothing will work out automatically unless you work towards it. The same applies to the prospect of growing in an organization.

8) As you grow in your career, it will be soft skills that will help determine your career path in a corporate environment; therefore, learn to be truthful and real with people.

LEARNING/ADVICE

Don't be afraid to take risks and chances if you think it would help your organization, but always discuss and take advice from your seniors.

Growth will only come to you if you are seeking it, and nothing will happen automatically.

As you grow in your career, it will be your soft skills that will determine your career in a corporate environment; therefore, learn to be truthful and real with people.

CHAPTER SIX

ENTREPRENEURSHIP

Today, while it seems that almost everybody is an entrepreneur and would like to own their own business, it was a very difficult decision for me to make that decision at the age of 40, even though I was probably ready for it around five years earlier; but my thought-process and the fact that almost everybody at home used to work for the government meant that my risk-taking ability had become quite subdued.

Having finally realized that it was something that I must do, I was prepared to give it everything. To take this decision, you must be ready to bear the consequences. Even though starting a business might seem easy, turning it into a successful organization and taking care of thousands of people takes everything. The success of any business depends on providing a return for all stakeholders and this means you must add value to your consumers without which it would be impossible for any business to survive. Maintaining the edge in consumer service is always easier said than done and that is mostly because of the ever-changing needs and demands of consumers and customers.

Any successful business needs a vision and goal which could add value to their customers and help the economy; it also requires a good team who can implement all necessary factors to achieve the entrepreneur's vision. In the end, the one thing which truly makes the difference in terms of a successful and not-so-successful business is the hunger of the leadership team to achieve their goals. In the race to achieve those goals, everyone must keep in mind the needs of customers, otherwise the enterprise will result in failure.

Entrepreneurship is not always easy. It is full of bumps at every step of the way and unless you are able to raise enough capital and your business plan is strong enough to weather the storm, it may not work.

Everything has to be right for creating a successful business—a right product that consumers want, a hardworking and ethical team, the right networking sources, support of your shareholders, the correct sales strategy, support of legislation, and above all, proper implementation.

While I would like to encourage everybody to try and become an entrepreneur and enjoy their own amazing experience, there are certain things that you need to do and be aware of which I have outlined as follows:

1) When choosing a product or service, you must decide on the one that the society thinks it wants but does not know how to get. This is the most basic factor that you should consider. You should ensure to find a niche in the market and find a way to differentiate your business against any competitors in the market. Once you get your base set in the market, you can then look for ways to expand your business.
2) You must come up with ideas which cannot be copied easily so you can have a *first mover advantage* for some time.
3) Once you have a vision and goal set, you must ensure to onboard a great team who believe in the same vision and have the right skill set and desire to help you achieve it. Along with this, you must ensure to acquire the shared interests of your shareholders and investors. In order to be a successful company, you must strive every step of the way to be patient as not every company may become an instant success. Therefore, when looking for investors, ensure to pitch creatively to those who can

help finance your business from the early stage till it becomes independent enough. To be a successful company, it takes years of hard work and it could be several years before your company becomes profitable; therefore, it is important to have investors who have deep pockets and are ready to support the company without profits till it becomes successful.

4) Before launching your products and services, it is essential to study your market and the needs of your target audience. Before you go big, it is important to acquire leads and test your product and make any changes, if needed. It is very important to know who could be among your primary clients and ensure that your product or service meets a clearly defined need.

5) The next step is to have a motivated sales team as, without a motivated team, you may not be able to make a sizable impact on the market. This is one of the key factors to the success of any business. A motivated sales team that is well compensated would go a long way in making the company successful.

6) You should initially map the demand and subsequent scaling of your business. Therefore, you should look for funding that could help you along the way in making your dreams come true while, at the same

time, adding value to society by creating efficiencies and jobs opportunities.

LEARNING/ADVICE

A sound vision that helps meet a certain demand or provides services required by consumers with various actionable goals and implementations are some of the inherent requirements for setting up and the eventual success of any business.

At the same time, I must say that entrepreneurship is a beautiful experience, and if you have a unique idea and are ready to give it everything to make it successful, you should certainly give it a try.

CHAPTER SEVEN

PARTNERSHIPS

When I was involved in the process of developing various businesses, one of the most important decisions revolved around having the right stakeholders and partnerships with the companies. As an entrepreneur, there are various partnerships that you must maintain and all of them are essential for the success of a business.

The first partnership would be to hire someone who shares your vision in helping make your business dream a reality. For example, you might be a product specialist focused on a new tech-product but be an introvert, in which case you would need an extrovert who could do sales for you and find the right clients for the product or services. Other partners you may need would be able to help you raise the funds needed to make your dream a reality. It is a process that could take time because it is not always easy to find the right partners who can fill in the gaps as well as those whose chemistry could work with you. This can be tricky and can either make or break a company. Therefore, it would be very important to discover your operating partnerships by evaluating your differences and defining a common goal. You can strengthen your partnerships with clearly-defined roles and nurturing mutual respect.

The second important partnership which will define the future of the company is having the right financial partner(s). It is important to have a financial partner who would understand the risk and rewards of investing in your business. It helps in staying fully transparent and in presenting a realistic plan to the investors. Many of the projects might require a long-term investment for them to be profitable; therefore, prior information on the same, discussed with potential investors, would be the ideal way to go. A frank discussion on the risks, rewards, timing, reporting, rights, and obligations at the very start would help you, as an entrepreneur, to focus on developing and driving the business while helping the investor to feel confident and secure about his investment.

Among all these partnerships, the one—if not the most critical one—that would decide the success or failure of your business is your clients or customers for your product and services. This is a partnership which takes time to build but will have a long-lasting effect on your business and ultimately affects how fast your business is going to grow and how quickly you could potentially become profitable. Nurturing a client is a very important part of the entire process, particularly in today's competitive market. Fulfilling a customer's product or service demands, in a timely and cost-effective manner, goes a long way to developing loyal customers.

Your own team should be ready to work with you day and night to make your dream come true. This is a very important partnership we need to have as entrepreneurs. For the success of the organization, it is important that they feel that they are part of the goals of the company and of its success. Hiring personnel with the right skills and getting an experienced team who will be loyal to the vision and goal of the organization is an extremely important determinant for the success of any venture. In my experience, one of the most important divisions for any organization is its sales and marketing team. Generating sales is an art, but the most important factor is to make sure your customer is happy with your product or services, which, in the end, is the only way you can survive in this competitive world.

The art of selling to and maintaining clients is a very important skill and a rare commodity. It is critical to carefully choose your sales team and along with their skill sets and drive, with their experience level being paramount.

In conclusion, partnerships are a make-or-break element of any enterprise, and it is essential to ensure that sufficient time and effort is invested into this aspect of the business at the earliest stage.

LEARNING/ADVICE

A key for you is to always keep your focus on your goals and keep taking small steps towards them.

It does not help to procrastinate; setting actionable goals and building important partnerships to move towards your goal would ultimately lead to the creation of a successful organization.

CHAPTER EIGHT

ENTREPRENEURSHIP'S REWARDS AND PITFALLS

Entrepreneurship is not only about starting a new business but is also a skill or talent that can be found among leaders in many modern organizations. With the rapid expansion of available information and skills through the internet, millennials today are daring to take risks at an early age and are working towards becoming entrepreneurs. They are always working towards creating the next Unicorn.

Since I began working over 25 years ago, the world has shifted dramatically. You cannot recognize a workplace today compared with when I first began, and in my opinion, it is going to change even more in the next 25 years.

The way that a business is conducted has shifted, and we are going to experience even greater shifts. What does this mean for all the experience that we have already acquired? Will it still be relevant? Of course, the fundamentals will remain the same, it is the methods that are going to keep on changing. The main pillar will still be that whatever you choose to do, it must be beneficial for your clients or customers, and you must engage in rigorous planning and hard work every step of the way. Your sales will need to be excellent and you will have to possess sound financial strength along with a disciplined approach towards your business. So, good planning, hard work, great sales efforts, sound financial strength and discipline are some of the factors that can help make it all work.

In this age, we see daily changes; however, real groundbreaking developments are hard to recognize and may take around ten to fifteen years before we see their true value emerge, as incremental innovations lead us to a place where we can look back and appreciate the work that was done. For example, the GPS tracker was developed more than a decade ago and is now leading the main feature of autonomous self-driving vehicles.

One of the pitfalls of being an entrepreneur is trying to become rich by doing business without thinking about how you are going to out-maneuver your competition and add value to your customers and society, at large. If your only objective is to make money in any way possible then it may be self-fulfilling; however, it may not work or create success in the medium to long term.

Risk taking is a fundamental attribute of entrepreneurs, along with vision and the ability to think differently. Hard work and soft skills are among the basic requirements. For you to attain success and make your vision come true, which may ultimately lead to wealth creation for you and your stakeholders, there are many things that must fall into place. Entrepreneurs go through many self-doubts along their way and may experience success, but the real reward is a great sense of self-satisfaction.

Pitfalls abound—long hours can affect your health and family life; it can even take a toll on your mental health. It is, therefore, essential to ensure that you have a schedule where you are doing physical exercise and making time for your family. Ego is quite prevalent, especially in the digital media age and it can be a big challenge to our relationships with our friends, colleagues, and family. Personal health, the right exercise, and eating well must be a top priority, even though they are difficult to manage while trying to develop your business. Getting your partners involved in these areas will be extremely useful to keep your health and ego in check. Entrepreneurs from different age groups will obviously face different challenges, and it is not the same for all.

Mental health is a popular topic in today's business world and attracts much discussion. I firmly believe that meditation is excellent to maintain productivity and overcome challenges at home and at work. If your business struggles or fails, you will go through many difficulties and face pain on all fronts—personal and professional. Do not feel disheartened. Recognize that you must learn from your mistakes, gather your energy, and dive deep into your passion again, only this time with more skills and experience. Learning from your mistakes is a key experience that no business course or book can teach you. You become wiser from these mistakes and I am very convinced that, if you keep a balanced mindset, you will never give up trying until you succeed.

Becoming successful can also be a pitfall. Surprisingly, you will certainly find that you have a lot more friends than you had before; however, it is important not to lose your state of mind. If you become proud or start thinking that all your friends really like you as a person, it will probably be far from reality. People may just be appreciating your success and may or may not be thinking of you as the person. You may find that the people who talk with you in a tough way are better well-wishers than those who talk to you with smooth, fine-sounding words.

In the end, whether you fail or succeed, it is important to be honest with your stakeholders and to not forget to provide the truth, love, and praise to the people that you value and help them to grow.

Keep your focus on your goals and always keep taking small steps forward.

LEARNING/ADVICE

It's important to understand we must be ready to undergo a certain amount of pain to achieve what we want in our life and we must accept challenges if we want to grow.

Entrepreneurship is challenging and has many pitfalls, but the learnings that one gets from it elevate our experiences of life.

CHAPTER NINE

MANAGING GROWTH

Hard work alone will not always be sufficient. We need to have help. Partnerships and the right team are essential if we wish to achieve growth after the initial set up. Sometimes, in our eagerness to have faster growth, we ignore strategy or the creation of everyday systems which would eventually help us with growth and maintenance. Think out of the box, as they say, and think big then take incremental steps towards your goal.

In managing growth, the first and more significant key is to have the right team. Here, you should go for the available people, and this may not always mean the best skill but rather the person with the right attitude, honest, and with a hunger to be successful. They must have the right character along with many of the skills for the job as possible.

Any business manager, CEO, or entrepreneur will tell you that getting the right team is the most difficult task that we must face. A lot of it is dependent upon the location where you are starting your business. You have probably heard many stories about Jeff Bezos starting his business in Seattle so that he could be close to Microsoft's head office, as he believed it would be easier for him to hire great talent. There is a certain reason why you will see that businesses are quite successful in certain cities and areas; this is because of the concentration of talent in that area and that applies both to living conditions and the business environment. Having said that, technology is helping to slowly create a level playing field.

Having hired the right talent, it is important to manage them well and keep them inspired. This can be done by providing them with the right conditions in which to perform their work and providing continual encouragement so that they can give their best to your business. This is easier said than done, primarily because every person's requirements are different. There are many books written by successful entrepreneurs explaining the theories of motivation—one common thread in those books is that a majority of people want to know what is in it for them when they help you achieve your goal. Crucially, your leadership qualities are going to play an important role here—Can you excite them? Can you lead them by example? Can you get them to believe in your dream? If you can do this, you will help them as they go along your journey together.

With the ongoing significant developments in technology, it doesn't matter what business you are in, technology will be integrated into your life, and when it comes to marketing and sales to grow your business or to establishing systems and procedures, you must keep these solutions in mind. This will ensure that while you are growing your business, the processes you employ will work smoothly and it will assist you in managing both your internal (employees) and external stakeholders (customers, government, regulatory bodies, shareholders, and the like). While building systems and using technology are expenses, they go a long way to making sure your company grows at the pace you would like to and that your business is secure from various problems it could be beset with for lack of those tools.

Investment in technology is critical, and at the same time, it can be costly too. It is a challenging decision for you and the shareholders to maintain the right balance. Investments versus cash burn is a difficult balancing act for all start-ups and this is influenced by how much cash was raised at the outset or the capital allocation decisions to cover the various expenses you might have. While it is easy for me to talk about it here, in reality, this becomes the crux for a cash burning business where the top management and board are hesitant to spend cash on such processes and technology, but this will ultimately be the limiting factor for your company's growth. There is no easy solution for this Catch 22 situation. Some entrepreneurs manage it by leading growth in the form of small increments, which in today's business might mean losing business or losing out to your customers.

Finally, it must be said that planning and strategy encompass all these elements and is the key determinant in the final success. It would be important to think of all the variables of the business and there should always be a plan to manage all relevant situations. Thinking ahead is key, and this is again something that is easier said than done, as every entrepreneur thinks that he knows best about his products or services. Therefore, it is good to build different scenarios and do a sensitivity analysis. Obviously, the visionary must depend upon instinct, but at the same time it is wise to take decisions based upon data, particularly that the world is changing rapidly, and your experience may not lead to relevant results. I personally think that instincts are important, however I also feel that decisions based upon proper data and embracing the views of senior management will be helpful, and even more when things are complex. One can always fine tune an institution by staying informed about the decisions that employees are taking and their eventual outcomes. This is where the proper systems in place are helpful.

To scale effectively one has to keep his persona and team's needs subservient to the organizational goals. Many times, such conflict of interest owing to personal needs or greed can arise and destroy the entire business. Therefore, constantly reinforcing the enterprise's commitment and helping managers adopt a goal focused mind-set will protect the business. Open and constructive communication creates a growth culture. It is sometimes easier to achieve in smaller businesses, but the challenge is to maintain it as you grow. Scaling up for an organization is a very challenging task which has many implications for you as the founder, your team and your organization. As the leader, if you can create and set goals, have the right management team and regulate some of your visionary tendencies, and try to grow in increments, there is certainly a greater likelihood of you being successful.

LEARNING/ADVICE

While all of us like to have growth in all fields including our personal and professional life,
what is important is for us to make sure we are ready for it when we get it.

Hard work and luck might favor you with growth but if you haven't planned well for sustainable growth with all its various variables, managing and maintaining it might be more challenging.

CHAPTER TEN

FINANCING

Once you have finalized a business idea, one of the most important things you have to do is to find ways to finance that idea into a reality. But the challenge lies in creating a great pitch deck that would help convince a reliable investor.

If it is your first venture in the cut-throat world of business, I would recommend taking help from a financial consultant who is experienced in raising funds for venture capital businesses or new enterprises. In such cases, ordinary corporate finance or investment banking advisors may not be able to help as much.

In your pitch deck, ensure to include a backstory that will engage your investors from the first meeting. Your product or service should be able to solve an existing problem that the current market or its consumers are facing. You should ensure to hold mock presentations and gain the approval of your advisors or colleagues. After your concise pitch deck that provides all the necessary information in brief is approved, you can then present it in front of your investors. But you should be confident in your speech. As an entrepreneur, after you have a business idea, one of the things that comes to your mind is, "How are you going to finance that idea?" Every entrepreneur who wants to start a new business, always thinks he has a great business idea, but the problem is for him to convince the investors that the idea really is a good one. If it's your first venture, again I would strongly recommend you take help from a financial consultant who has experience raising funds for Venture Capital businesses/new enterprises and not normal corporate finance/investment banking advisors. While you might have a great idea and vision of doing something, please always remember not to forget, "Is this idea beneficial for consumers?" and, "What problems are you going to solve for them?" If you think after discussing with your friends and the advisor that the idea is helpful and would be in demand, then prepare an elevator pitch of say 1 to 2 minutes.

Like I said at the start, I am going to mention it again, it is extremely wise to avail the services of an advisor, and certainly if you have no prior experience of raising capital for businesses. I must clarify here that we are talking about a new venture, you could be working with individuals or groups of individuals who may not be part of a large corporate or existing fund-raising experience.

The first type of investors includes those who mainly fund start-ups and are known as Angel or Smart Investors. They are high-net worth individuals and differ from normal investors in their ability to take high risks as well as to wait for the returns on their investment. When selecting to pitch to an investor, you must check their risk-return profile as it makes a huge impact on the performance of the new venture. This is because undue pressure on the new venture to make profits will put significant pressure on the company and could potentially lead to its failure. Angel investors and Smart Investors differ from normal investors in their ability to take higher risk as well as their ability to wait for the returns.

It's important to understand from the financial advisor how to build up the pitch and try to be as authentic as possible as that would help the advisor to choose the investors who would suit your business the most. Once you know the investor it's very important to do your homework, and preparation is the key. The pitchbook that you have, apart from the elevator pitch, has to be perfect in terms of how it presents your story in an attractive manner. Please always get professional help. This is going to be your first impression on the investor, therefore, to make sure that it's not the last one, it's therefore absolutely crucial that they are well thought out and professional. You should always be ready with your detailed business plans and financial model. In the current times don't hesitate to use a digital presentation or video of your product which could be pretty attractive for your investors. You have to just make sure whichever format you use, it is engaging and informative.

Luckily in today's digital era finding angel/venture investors is not that difficult but preparing the right pitch desk which will excite the investor is certainly a challenge. Therefore, it's important to know your investor beforehand and what attracts him the most. Also, it's important to find different methods of fundraising than just looking at the traditional way which I have been suggesting before. In the current age things like crowdfunding are getting very popular as a way of fundraising for your new venture. I don't want to recommend any crowdfunding site, but every year billions of dollars get raised through these sites. The first place you should start before getting into Angels and so on, would be to tap into family and friends and see what they think about your vision, and find out if they would give you the start-up capital. Some of the other kinds of investors who could be very interested in your new venture could be people who would consume your products or services, depending on what your plans are.

Sometimes bigger companies might also be interested to make a strategic investment into your product or services if you belong to a particular industry, and they might want to partner with you. If you have such an idea, reach out to them directly for such a partnership.

Many governments around the world have set up various incubation programs which help start-ups though mostly for start-ups in the tech field, and similar initiatives are done by various foundations, all depending on what problem you are trying to solve. For example, many governments are ready to fund research and development (R&D) for technology or healthcare development start-ups, and the same is true for innovations in the education sector.

While you look for financing it's important to make sure that the legal structure is right, even before you start the process. Investors will certainly focus on the legal structure and this is how you assure that your vision and hard work is suitably rewarded. Apart from you putting in the capital yourself, investors don't mind giving extra shares which get vested on achieving various milestones. But having the right legal framework would give you and investors a better peace of mind, and that would allow you more time to focus on developing your business without being worried about regulatory constraints or issues.

In short there are many different kinds of investors that we have discussed, you need to decide who you will focus on, it could be your family & friends, angel investors, smart investors, big industry players, government start-up programs, foundations, crowdfunding sources and so on. There are of course several start-up and venture capital funds, incubators and private accelerators which could also be helpful.

LEARNING/ADVICE

Every idea needs funding to be able to realize its true potential and in today's environment this might be one of the most challenging things to accomplish.

A unique idea which is helpful to solve problems for the masses will always find funding, and today both the government and private sector are supporting such developments.

The key is to get the right advice early on.

CHAPTER ELEVEN

MANAGING CHANGE

We all know that change is the only constant in life. Despite that we all get afraid and most of the time worried when we have to embrace change. Accepting this factor is all part of your life as an entrepreneur. History is full of examples where entrepreneurs began building something, then where they failed or had to change their course mid-way, they then went on to be hugely successful. Therefore, while going through your own trials, ideas and failures all you need is to believe in your dreams, prepare well, but always be ready to change course in case things don't go your way. But never leave your dreams.

My relationship with change has been a very consistent and fruitful one and has helped me when changing cities, moving between countries, and making friends all over the world; and in getting help to invest or set up many businesses in different cities. But in the short stint of only 15 years from starting or heading businesses or my entrepreneurship of 10 years it has become clear that what worked 15, 10 or even 3 years back, is not going to work now. Therefore, my old experience, unlearning what made the earlier businesses successful, studying for an MBA, working in various companies, all came in handy and contributed to my successes. I am sure all successful entrepreneurs have gone through similar experiences where they have had to unlearn their earlier strategy, figure out new marketing and new practices to bring them in line with the current requirements, changed customer expectations, as well as a changed business environment.

There were many times during the last several years where I had to scrap the whole idea on which we were working and change the business plan and start afresh. Practically I have always tried to keep myself apace with developments by trying to work with people of different ages and different experiences or varied skill sets. It has helped me a great deal in keeping myself ahead in terms of learning and planning things better. It always makes you feel uneasy early on, but this discomfort also helps to disrupt your routine, inspire ideas, eliminate superficial thinking and help to create something better than I could ever achieve alone. In fact, I know of many celebrities and people who try to create superficial suffering or change which would help them to think better and think new, this is one way of observing growth through a change in reality.

Undergoing many failures is a part of life, and, as an entrepreneur, I have developed a habit to manage these changes and find a better version of myself. Some of the ways in which I have tried to manage changes in my life is to stay agile and remain quick and flexible with the decisions that I make and trust my instincts.

Technology in terms of digital media has become the most important channel today for somebody to market his products or services. It is, therefore, important for anybody who wants to survive and flourish today, that his business continually adapts to the fast-changing marketing and selling dynamics and adopt the new methods of digital media and forget the old way of conducting business. I emphasize, this deconstruction of the business model is very important to survival in the current competitive environment.

It is usually fear which stops us from taking that leap of faith, making that change. The greatest obstacle against transforming ourselves is the nagging worry that we will buckle under the emotional strain that comes with big changes. I have handled these changes by trying to keep myself aware of the current environment, disrupting things only incrementally and taking small steps.

My final say is that the life of an entrepreneur is exciting, full of risk and exceptional learning experiences. There is no substitute for putting everything on the line and seeing something that you have created impacting the lives of your customers, your team and your shareholders and investors. it is stimulating and a dynamic place to be.

My final thought is this: "Everybody needs to decide for themselves".

LEARNING/ADVICE

It's being afraid of change which always holds back our evolution and growth.

Change triggers many different emotions in all of us.

Accepting change and adopting a positive attitude will go a long way in making us a better version of ourselves.

CHAPTER TWELVE

HOW TO START A NEW BUSINESS

This is obviously one of the hottest topics these days which is the focus of the young, old and the governments. During the pandemic it actually takes more center stage as the gigantic amount of job losses can only be solved through creation of new and successful businesses which meet the needs of the society. This is of course easier said than done with new start-ups, with their success rate being very low, which could be for many reasons starting from lack of proper vision or idea to lack of focus or discipline, to being not to in the right place/ city, to not having the right connections or the right funding in place.

I am sure you can find many different ways to start a new business and run it successfully through the internet these days. Having gone through starting around 8-10 businesses in the last 15 years, I will share with you my personal experiences, what worked for me, and if something didn't work, why it didn't. The most difficult thing about a start-up is that it's your vision as founder and nobody else's, therefore, it's important that the vision be such that your team members and other stakeholders are able to envision themselves being a part of and believing in the same. And that is the only way everybody can be aligned to achieve the goals of the new business/start-up.

Another very important aspect would be goal setting at the start, which is then broken down into smaller objectives to be achieved. This would certainly involve forming a business plan which should constitute the detailed plans for the new business, and a study of the industry, competition, market, financial projections, etc. But again, the key differentiating factor I have seen which makes the difference between a success and failure has been my focus on a particular business and details. Trying to create many businesses might help in creating jobs but if not led by the right leader and lack of alignment of interest would mean a failed business with shareholder value destruction. Therefore, it's very important to have a business which you love and can concentrate and focus upon as if it's the only thing you have. Having a great team is equally important but the skill set needed for a start-up is rare as the talent pool is limited. Therefore, to have the right team, which is focused on making your vision come true, has the right skill set, and has the alignment of interest, is imperative for any start-up business to reach success.

Even if you have all the above elements, the success of a start-up would depend on how the founder is able to market his project to investors so that he can raise the necessary capital to make his dream a reality. It must be marketed in a way that it's easy for anybody who listens to the pitch to understand in the first 5 minutes, some might say in the first minute itself.

The other important factor is to prepare well, but at the same time if there are disappointments on the way, never give up. Use the experience and improve the business model. If you have to take risks along the way to seize opportunities, you should certainly do that. Creating something new is always difficult at the start but when done correctly it is very rewarding. Therefore, for success it's essential that we focus on creating rather than complaining about obstacles. Rather we should use those obstacles to create opportunities. I have always believed that obstacles create unique opportunities for us which otherwise we might have ignored. The key word here would be the focus that we as entrepreneurs need to have on our businesses to make them successful, so that every moving part of the business is managed well. One of the most important parts of that business model is to build a customer centric business which meets the needs of consumers as well as being value for money for them.

These ideas and thoughts have many sub processes and lead to extensive activities that must follow, but the most important is to act, even if it leads to failure. Some of the most important guidelines to follow are to understand that every business has inherent risks and if you are afraid of risks then it's better to work for somebody as a professional and have a great career, you don't necessarily need to start a business. An entrepreneur usually would see every obstacle as an opportunity.

When we start a business, we should always remain focused on success, but you should know that there could be short term failures, we must learn from them, analyze them and adapt new appropriate strategies. Usually not taking enough risks means we are not adopting new ways of thinking or innovating. New ways and taking risks in the long run may be more helpful for building successful business even though in the short term they might lead to losses and failures. While going through these trials it's required for us to remain positive; starting a new business is not something for the faint hearted to do, it means you are already way ahead of others who have decided to pursue a less risky path.

LEARNING/ADVICE

Goal setting at the start is very important
to properly plan a new business set up which can then be broken down into smaller goals/objectives to achieve.

As an Entrepreneur it's normal for you to face many obstacles but maintaining a positive mindset and finding solutions will go a long way in building a successful Business.

CHAPTER THIRTEEN

POWERFUL HEALTH PRACTICES FOR ENTREPRENEURS

Start-ups and Entrepreneurship are some of the hottest topics these days and almost every government around the world is trying to promote these ventures as they substantially increase job creation for the economies, thereby helping in poverty reduction. People immerse themselves in entrepreneurship with a dream of creating something unique as per their thoughts which when created would give them immense personal satisfaction. It helps them take control of their life and also helps them in their personal development. Frequently entrepreneurs suffer, while it gives them the opportunity to drive their own life and follow their dreams, it can also lead to many unhealthy practices like the long hours they have to put in, unpredictable workflows, all driven by a do or die attitude. This can be a very stressful experience for many entrepreneurs at the early stage of their life, particularly if they don't have the right financial or family support.

It is also true that as entrepreneurs we might have disappointment in life, but how we manage those is what will define us. Entrepreneurism can lead not only to negative health issues but also mental problems, so entrepreneurs and start-up owners must learn how to manage their health effectively so that they can lead the growth of their business. It's important to keep in mind the truth that only a healthy body and mind can take the pressures of a hectic daily life and sustain growth during both good times and bad times. The life of an entrepreneur is not defined by linear growth, usually it will always lead to disappointment or lack of something in life.

Now like Investments, there is no magic strategy which fits all. Obviously depending on your age and your condition (if you have any ailment etc.) there will be different strategies that a nutritionist or doctor might recommend for you. Myself being a type 2 diabetes, with lactose and gluten intolerance I know a bit about ailments and with all the stress of start-ups, I can enumerate the steps that I have taken which have helped me in keeping sanity during the time when everything starts going south because a business or venture is not doing well, like many new ventures might be undergoing during these difficult pandemic times.

The simplest and most basic way to keep a healthy body and mind can start with doing physical exercise, as it not only helps our body, but it also substantially helps our mind and thinking. The pain and suffering you receive during these physical exercises will help you start thinking differently. There are many different recommendations (a google search will provide plenty!) or from doctors who would tell you why scientifically it helps you to relax and helps your thinking pattern. I try to exercise at least 3 times a week even though it might be far removed from the 5 days I would like to do because of my erratic work times. Depending on your age and the metabolism rate your body has it might not be very helpful for you to lose weight, but it might be helpful for you to do some weight training to keep the muscles tight and the right muscle-fat proportion. One way of tricking your body to burn fat to produce energy instead of carbohydrate is to use something known as bulletproof coffee (if coffee suits your body, otherwise you can try the same with tea as well) or different variants of the same. I have learnt that eating well and clean food would mean a strong body, and which ultimately will lead to a healthy mind.

I have learnt a few ways where food has worked to keep my body and mind healthy during the most difficult situations despite being diabetic. I can enumerate some of the steps which could be easy to follow. I take as many fruits as I feel like, but only in the morning, in a way that is the only sweet

I would prefer during the day. I try my best not to have any fruits beyond 12 pm in the afternoon. Also, usually I eat 3-4 times a day and try not to restrict myself from anything that I like to eat while trying to avoid gluten and lactose. But I have tried to discipline myself not to have any food beyond 6pm except maybe a vegan protein with some Maca powder before 7 p.m. (I do have a cheat day when I go out for dinner once a week). Of course, drinking 2-3 liters of water during the day has been a usual ritual with me for a long time now. Like everything, always keep simple principles which are easy to follow. I have different ways of relaxing like watching serials and movies, cooking, shopping and reading.

I have observed that an active lifestyle and clean food habits is insufficient for a peaceful and happy mind, especially since I struggle to sleep beyond 5 or 6 hours a day. What has helped me considerably is my 15 to 20 minutes of meditation everyday (it has taken me a few years to reach this level, having started at hardly 5 minutes at the start). Apart from all the above, I think what excites me also despite all the depression and negativity I might go through for a few days is to think of doing something new and exciting in terms of work. That works as a perfect antidote which always keeps the adrenaline flowing, but I believe an active lifestyle, clean food and meditation are the things which help me in keeping my sanity and remaining focused on my goals.

LEARNING/ADVICE

Entrepreneurship comes with its
own challenges
and foremost among them is to
maintain mental equilibrium
and good health conditions.

As an Entrepreneur it's important
for us to maintain
an active lifestyle and keep
ourselves both physically and
mentally fit
for us to give 100% to our
projects to make them successful.

CHAPTER FOURTEEN

START-UP

Now, this is something very close to my heart. Start-ups in the last 20–25 years have become almost a fad, and everybody wants to do a start-up. I am actually very encouraged by the fact that this is happening which shows that all of us are trying to innovate and try and make different products or provide differentiated services. This idea of being independent and self-employment is also a great idea as it helps in improvement of the employment rate and self-sustainability of the economies. Having done this almost 10 years back and every time doing it repeatedly. For me it's like an adrenalin to see your dream, your ideas coming true. Because usually for an entrepreneur it's usually his idea and to be frank while some might appreciate it if it helps in solving a problem faced by most population otherwise most and usually don't care about your ideas and dreams. That is the first shock that one should expect as an entrepreneur and should come to appreciate that nobody else believes in his dream unless they can really make money out of it which comes only a few years down the years. I certainly felt talking to the walls some 10 years back sitting in a 50 sq ft small room alone for 6 months. I must say I was very lucky that having done some may be 400-500 calls and maybe 100s of meetings, I was able to convince at least 7 investors who could believe in my idea and decided to support me in my initial endeavor. I am always very thankful to those individuals who took the initial risk with me and supported the idea.

I consider myself very lucky because I know several entrepreneur's during the same period and later too tried to raise capital for their start-up, but either were not successful or had to give up their dream in between. Because the process of capital raising is an extremely difficult process and could be very frustrating as investors usually end up believing in only what they see and not an idea and a business plan that you may have. But I also totally understand that taking risk with seed capital is not everybody's palate as the risk return profile of those investors is very different and therefore, we need to be very choosy as a start-up to decide who we should be pitching our idea to. If you are not in the USA but anywhere else in the world, you are already at a disadvantage with respect to your idea since I believe a majority of the capital is already directed towards only that one country. But we have to admire the different developments and innovations which have come out from that country and have helped in reshaping the world with its various innovations and brilliant ideas by the entrepreneur's resident in that country.

Now coming back to the Middle East, I must say that anybody staying and trying to do start-ups in UAE also has quite an advantage compared to many other nearby countries because of the quality of life, work culture and eco environment set up here which attracts the best talent from many countries. Therefore, UAE becomes a big enabler in that sense. Having said that, ultimately it would depend on the entrepreneur himself and his team to be able to sell their start-up and themselves to the investors and other stakeholders equally. The difficulties with start-ups are that most start-ups fail and burn a lot of money and that is the fact of life. But it's also true that those who survive actually thrive in a big way and make up for all the losses that investors might have made elsewhere.

But it's very important that the entrepreneur has to plan the kind of investors he takes in as somebody who is not used to investing in new businesses and doesn't understand the start-up philosophy can actually kill the whole business and make it very difficult for the start-up team to run their business. Because making the start-ups successful takes a long time and most of the investors don't have patience for the same. On the other hand, you might have a family who may not also understand why you are putting in long hours at work while you don't make much in terms of financial matters at the early stages of the venture. It could affect your health as well as your mental state going through those trying times. Therefore, make sure your resolve to be successful is unwavering and you plan well.

In summary, let's go through some simple steps that a start-up would need to have:

1) An idea and a vision which would help meet a certain demand/need of the society/consumers.
2) Work on a detailed business plan which would constitute developing your idea into a full-blown product/service constituting features of your product/services, demand-supply, industry, competition, marketing strategy/go to market, financial projections etc.
3) SOP for each important department like strategy, marketing, finance, manufacturing/production, etc.
4) Having the elevated speech ready and organizing proper fund-raising rounds.
5) It's important simultaneously to find the right partner/team members who can complement your skill set.

6) Have an office space where the team can work together would be nice, but if you can't afford one still it's good. as unless you are into manufacturing almost all business and mostly services can be carried out from home, coworking spaces, coffee shops, etc.
7) Just remember having the best product/services is not enough to develop a successful venture, unless you have a great marketing/sales team which can make your product/service a success.
8) Before you start marketing the idea/product/services, make sure to test its viability, listen to customer feedback and make sure you have a winnable product.
9) To top all the above make sure you never give up your dream.

LEARNING/ADVICE

If You think you have a great idea which would help solve a problem for an issue faced by a large population, then you have the right idea for a startup.

But to convert the idea to a successful business
you need to take action, which will go a long way to making you a successful Entrepreneur.

Shailesh Dash

Award winning Entrepreneur, Ideator, Mentor, and Philanthropist

Coming from a humble background in the small city of Puri from Odisha in India, I have come a long way by building successful businesses in the Gulf, while raising multi-billion-dollar funds for various corporations as well as working on new business venture ideas and bringing them to fruition.

I love what I do. I believe my purpose in life is to create successful businesses and take great ideas and turn them into valuable, profitable entities. My core belief is based upon adding value to society through increasing employment opportunities and improving financial literacy to make as many people financially independent as humanly possible.

Shailesh is a professional business advisor and is able to assist in providing directions and insights for entrepreneurs.

Drop him an email to shailesh@sdash.net and he will get back to you.

You can do it when you want to!

NOTES:

www.ingramcontent.com/pod-product-compliance
Lightning Source LLC
Chambersburg PA
CBHW070805220526
45466CB00002B/555